T0068180

MENTALLY
DISABLING PAIN

Physically, Mentally, Emotionally

BORNE MALIK SANDERS

authorHOUSE®

AuthorHouse™
1663 Liberty Drive
Bloomington, IN 47403
www.authorhouse.com
Phone: 833-262-8899

Published by AuthorHouse 05/18/2021

ISBN: 978-1-6655-2662-3 (sc)
ISBN: 978-1-6655-2661-6 (e)

Library of Congress Control Number: 2021910214

To get a better understanding of me, allow me to take you back to my very first memory. All I saw were lab coats and nurses when my eyes opened again for the second start of my life. I remember this white man in a white lab coat telling this beautiful woman that "he" will have to relearn how to walk and talk again and "he" may not be able to completely walk properly ever. I wasn't certain what exactly he was referring to at the time, all I remember is the comfort I felt from seeing that beautiful woman by my hospital bed. That beautiful woman was my mother. Neurons reconfigured almost like a reboot and there was a thought that formed in my mind to ask why that pretty woman and other family members looked so sad, only the words came out like mush. Although these neurons were firing once again in my brain, I could not get my tongue muscles to pronounciate anything I was thinking. As days turned to weeks, I was able to somewhat piece together what happened. I suffered a traumatic head injury resulting in me losing all brain activity, mentally I was dead. All of this resulted from an attempt to do a backflip on high ground for the first time as a dare, only the ground was marble. I do not remember my exact age the incident occurred but deductive reasoning permits me to believe I had to be in elementary during this time period. Once home from the hospital I was sentenced to bed rest to the point rest became restlessness. When I thought the apartment was empty, I gave my legs a try at walking but every step I tried to take felt so jittery almost like I did squats till exhaustion and there was little to no power behind my leg muscles. I don't know if it was my brain or lack of leg muscles but I had to abort this restless attempt trying to grab on to anything I could before I fell. Somehow, I made it back to my bed.

I value you for reading my story but do not pity me as you will soon read, they're less than perfect thoughts that lead to consequences that can't be undone from me. Allow me to fast forward a little past my head injury as I do not have any memories before that. Not sure where we were but my mom drove us somewhere in her car given to her by my father. I was waiting in the car, seconds turned to minutes and those minutes felt like hours. Curiosity and boredom led me to discover some matches in the car, how could I resist? Over confidently I kept setting flame to a restaurant take out box and blowing out the flame before it got too big. I soon discovered that my lungs were not nearly as powerful as my curiosity for fire. Probably not to your surprise, the flame got too big forcing me to get out of the car as I watched it burn. All my elder family members gave me a whooping every time I saw them for a while. The worst came from my mother, she disciplined me and I did not dare to play with matches again in her next car.

Eventually my mind developed to the point where I gained freedom to play outside without supervision, but maybe someone should 'of been watching me because I ended up back in the hospital suffering a cut and concrete burn to my chin from falling off my bike. Surgery passed and I felt like I was awarded green stiches to my chin that were cool because they changed colors with time till they came out on their own. Once again healed thanks to the doctors, I was eager to get back outside. Reacquainted with my freedom of being outside playing again, I was reunited with the kids in my neighborhood. Every neighborhood has older kids and unfortunately for me they did not like me too well and not just the older ones. A kid a little younger than me did a backflip off a fence and dared me to follow up. Pressure set in for me to fit in so my mindset became competitive. Before I could even attempt another kid stopped me this time, not sure why. Looking back on the situation I wonder if he knew of my previous injury from attempting that stunt. An older kid gave it a try and failed miserably, no serious injuries though. I thought his failure was the most hilarious thing I ever seen and started a wave of infectious laughter, next thing you know everyone was laughing. This is where the joke ends for the older kid though, he lashed out at me swinging his fist in a mad rage only I easily dodged them. Giving up his attempts to punch me, he invited me and a couple others to play video games in his house. Confused but not wanting to go home out of an eerie thought that anger may spark again in my mother for burning her car, I went to play video games with my attacker. Almost everyday brought attempts from older kids wanting to fight me only I wasn't always able to avoid a beat down. A new day came and I was called outside to play by an older kid only this one did not have ill intent against me, or at least I thought. Today's adventure was in a tree, we climbed as high as our confidence allowed and another older kid came and set at the bottom of the tree, not interested in climbing. The other older kid I was in the tree with dropped a pinecone hitting the other older kid in the head and the kid that knocked on my door for me to come outside instantly blamed me for his doing. Believing I did a good job articulating that I did not throw the pinecone, I felt no fear to climb down the tree when I was ready to leave. My words were useless, soon as my feet touched the ground it felt like it was an earthquake in my head followed by a headache from, I don't know how many times that older kid punched me. Not really excited to be in the house due to mother's rage from my dumb actions of setting her car on fire and losing interest in being around anyone outside, school didn't seem like too bad of a place to waste time. Not to mention I was fairly decent in all subjects at school.

Not sure how I was given the position as just a kid but the basketball coach asked if I would like to be assistant coach for the girl's basketball team when I was in middle school. I did not care that I had no knowledge of how to assist, I just accepted the offer. I can't avoid my neighborhood though as one day some kids wanted to play basketball with me outside. The team I was on won and I even hit the game winning shot to end it. As me and the other kids were about to leave, one of them asked if I think I could beat Lesly. Feeling confident in my abilities from hitting the game winning shot I naturally replied yeah. That kid was not talking about basketball, as on my walk home Lesly asked me if I was the one who said I could beat him. I said yeah still thinking the topic was basketball. That kid was punching me with so much force that my jaw pops till this day when opened past a certain point. The only thing I could think while this older kid was punching my jaw off my henges is why doesn't he push me down this ditch. We were on the side walk and it was a very steep ditch to my right that I'm certain I would have been stuck in if I was to fall into it. To this day not sure if I knew I would lose is the reason I never struck back at the older kids or a hopeless idea that I would make friends. Over the period of time I've realized that all friends don't have honest intentions.

Taking enough beatings without fighting back, I would soon see how fast my hands were in comparison to others at my school in the form of slap boxing. In my eyes a completely harmless sport, but in the eyes of the teachers and the principal, well they saw differently. Some of my friends and I created fake gangs each based off the suit of cards in a deck, diamonds, spades, etc. I became leader of clovers and only accepted recruits if they won slap box tournaments we use to hold in the bathrooms. Not sure exactly how but word got out and next thing I know I'm being called to the principal office. I was asked if I was involved with fights occurring in the bathrooms. No punches were thrown and no blood was shed so I replied "no" with a conscious that we were slap boxing. I was forced to sit down and watch footage of me standing at the entrance of the bathroom doing a hand gesture resulting in other students running to come in the bathroom. Needless to say, I got suspended after watching that recording of me on camera. Great, I was thrown back to the older kids again. My very next memory I have is that of me at the beach and it must have been skip day or everyone was suspended because there was a lot of kids there. I naturally knew how to swim, don't remember being taught by anyone. I saw a group of older kids in deeper waters and instantly challenged myself to see if I could swim out that deep. Reaching where the big kids were, I felt part of their circle by treading water to keep my head above water just to be near them. An older kid moved towards me. I threw no pinecones, I didn't say I could beat anyone, and I did not laugh at anyone's downfall. I was certain I was going to make friends this time, wrong again. The older kid instantly put me in the headlock. His feet touched the sands of the ocean, I had to tread water to breath. Unable to free myself of his grip, he continuously dumped my head in and out of the ocean to the point where I could not tell when it was safe to try to inhale for air. I've reached my limit; I have to inhale. I took a big gasp; my timing was perfect as I realized water is not in my lungs. Another twenty seconds maybe of survival, I can't waste energy trying to escape his grip, there is no point. I gave up. Soon as I did, he must have lost interest because I did not feel his presence anymore. I swam to shore fast as I could thinking I have to become more agile in water. Some may have deterred away from water at that point, I was determined to become more cognitive of my movements in water and chose to go swimming any chance I could get.

Back at school once again. I was placed in advanced math, don't know how or why but there were not many other kids that resembled my skin complexion. In fact, there were only two black kids in that math class including myself and the other was a female. Every day before I could go outside to play my mom made me complete a page out of this math workbook. It soon came to the point where I was not completing the pages to go outside but because I actually enjoyed this new challenge of playing with numbers. One day finishing my page before my mom got home from work, I decided to go outside to check the mailbox. This older kid must have been playing cops and robbers with the younger ones because I spotted him chasing them around with what resembled a gun. Not interested in playing I turned to see and collect what was in the mailbox. When I collected everything and turned back to go home that older kid was maybe a couple feet in front of me, not interested in playing I continued to take a step in his direction towards my home. He raised the gun took aim at me; my only thought was that I'm not interested in running away playing his game. He pulled the trigger and shot me directly in the middle of my forehead with unwavering accuracy. The pellet got lodged partially in my skull leaving blood to trickle down my face to my lips allowing me to taste my blood for the first time. I made it back in the house to hear pandemonium from my cousin as she called my mom and aunt screaming, "Borne got shot!" I could only look in the mirror in amazement from his aim because if it were not true, I would be missing an eye at this point. Luckily only a pellet gun and not a real one, I found myself at the hospital to hear comical remarks that I must have a pretty hard head. This hospital visit was pretty short as I was reunited with my neighborhood once again in no time.

Back reunited with my friends, we discovered a way to get money to buy snacks and food from our corner store. We devised out of copper/metal hangers a way to collect quarters out of the car wash machine.

We had a system in place that whichever car was there while we were collecting quarters would get a free car wash. We became known as the quarter boys from stores we would go to buy food and exchange our quarters for bills. Doing our normal routine collecting quarters one day the squad took off running in the middle of our operation. I thought nothing of it and continued collecting assuming the car behind me was a regular who was with our system. I saw lights flash looked back and realized quickly it was a police officer. Taken downtown for questioning they held me there for awhile asking questions of which I was not 100% sure how to answer or exactly what they meant so I gave no responses. My mom later arrived with certificates and my A-B honor roll awards and the narrative became that I was simply in the wrong place at the wrong time with the wrong crowd and I was set free. Next thing I know I'm back at school and the day flew by so fast it seemed like I blinked and I was back on the bus on the way back home. Shortly arriving to my neighborhood, we heard gun shots, I looked out the window and saw two older kids shooting at each other and ducking behind cars. I watched momentarily heard my stomach growl and instantly thought what am I going to eat when I walk in the house. Getting off the school bus my arm was grabbed by this girl who said the shots made her so nervous she has to pee and begged that I let her in my house to use the bathroom. What? No, I replied, go to your own house. I may have been too young at the time to realize that maybe she was coming onto me because her apartment was literally next door. I would soon learn that there were gangs in my neighborhood and school but only notice red and blue bandanas outside of school. One of my friends got into a verbal altercation with someone else, started cursing him out and threw up gang signs after the argument was over. Not sure what they were arguing about, I just thought the signs he was throwing up was the coolest thing I've seen. One of the first parties I went to, I saw this kid with a red bandana and went up to him giving him a unique handshake that I learned from my other friend that was throwing up gang signs. After we did the unique handshake, he leaned to my ear and asked who's my OG? I replied, I don't bang I just rep, I think y'all cool as hell. Little did I know if I would have said the wrong thing, I would not have made it out that party in one piece. I noticed I was surrounded by others at that party with the same color bandanas and soon as I gave my response to the one I did the unique handshake with, he waved his hand and all the others wearing the red bandanas disappeared back into the crowd of the party. When the party ended me and some other kids walking home in the same direction after returning some bikes to the porches we stole from ending tonight's adventure, we heard car tires screech leaving skid marks from a black jeep. "Yo come here!" one of the guys from the jeep said. I was the only one to walk up to the jeep. The guy said, "Oh these ain't the niggas" and pulled off swerving. One of the kids that I was walking home with started laughing and said, "you almost walked into a bullet". How could one walk into a bullet I thought?

The next day after school I was hanging outside with some other kids and this older kid with a blue bandana came up to us with a CD player and told us to listen, so we took turns. This would be the spark that first got me interested in writing lyrics as the older kid told us it was him on the CD. The very next day a different kid in a blue bandana approached me and some kids I was with and stated that he liked my shoes. The other kid beside me started yelling at him to the point tears was coming out his eyes saying on my mama's grave this is not what you want. It appears I made a true friend. To explain things for those who may not understand, when a gansta say they like something of yours and you don't know them, it is not a compliment. It means they are going to beat you up and take it from you. The Crip looked at me again for a couple seconds started laughing then walked away.

Unfortunately, the true friends I did make did not last too long because my mom would get new jobs so I would be in and out of a couple different neighborhoods. Playing tag outside one day I ran in the house for snacks to refuel. Soon as I walked in the house my mom yelled, "what the hell is that!". I looked down and noticed I was leaving a trail of blood dripping from my left hand. "Damn Borne that looks deep enough for stitches", she said. I thought and said I don't need stitches I honestly don't even feel it. I was confused as hell though as to how I got the injury then it clicked when I thought about it. There was a rusty old washing machine by the dumpster outside and I remember running pretty close by it before

I made it to the house. When I ran by it, it must have sliced the backside of my hand open. My mom became my nurse that day and tended to my wound. Not feeling any pain, I felt no reason to stay inside so I ventured back out into the neighborhood. As the sun was starting to set, I was approached by this old drunk man who said he will give me twenty dollars if I can beat him in a race. I knew he was drunk because he reeked of alcohol. Little did he know I placed 3rd in first in fitness triathlon at school. Another kid said, "on your mark… get set… Go! I mean it wasn't even close, I completely embarrassed the old timer and took his money and left home. My mom had company over when I ran in the house. I completely interrupted whatever they were talking about excited to tell her what just happened. When her company left, I got another whooping. The lesson behind this one was to not call my elders some drunk old man. I was confused though because it was true so I thought she must still be mad at her first car I set on fire.

Today at school we were given catalogs that was a fund raiser to raise money for our school. The top three students that sold the most would get prizes at the school pep rally. Thinking to myself, I don't really feel like knocking on doors, I'm just going to give it to my mom. I explained to her what it was and she replied, "I'll make sure you win". When the time period ended and it was time to turn everything in there was a long waiting period for our class to get the results back. I dosed off and woke up to hearing my name being called as one of the top three who sold the most. My mom must have force everyone at her job to buy something. This must have got this cute white girl attention of me because the next day she asked me to be her boyfriend. This is the first girlfriend I had in middle school and everyday when she saw me, she would hug me so tightly I would have to pry her loose. Once the school day was over and I was on the school bus to go home, this black girl sat in the seat in front of me put her window down and turned and looked at me. "I want to be your girlfriend", she said. I already have a girlfriend I replied quickly. She burst out laughing, "no you don't and if you do, she's probably white". How do you know my girlfriend is white? She burst out laughing again, "Oh my God I was joking but its true!". So what?! I yelled. She laughed again and said you're an Oreo. I looked out the window and thought, Oreos are pretty good with milk, I think I'm going to eat cookies when I get in the house. The next day at school, lunch time came and my girlfriend gave me her lunch she brought from home saying you're going to love it and went in the lunch line to get lunch for herself. We finished eating and she said, "O.K. you have to carry my books for me because I'm your girlfriend". She kissed me once I walked her to her class then I went to my class. Unfortunately, I had to break up with her because yet again my mom got a new job resulting in me moving to another neighborhood.

This is the neighborhood where I made the transition from middle school to high school. My first interest was joining the football team. School had not quite started yet as it was still summer vacation. I got acquainted with the new school district I would be in and became a part of the football team overcoming the rigorous training schedule of two – a day football practices. There were a couple of days after we got shoulder pads that I made the hardest hit of the day securing a starting position on defense. Unfortunately, I would not be able to play to the full extent of my abilities. The reason being, one day after we made it through our first practice of the day, I decided to ride my bike back home to rest before it was time for our second practice of the day. Time elapsed and I got on my bike making it maybe halfway to practice before I decided to make a pit stop at the store for Gatorade. The store was at the bottom of a hill perpendicular to the parking lot. Going down the hill picking up momentum with each rotation of my tires, a car from the bottom of the hill leaving was heading directly in my path. Instantly I reached for my brakes, useless, I felt no decrease in speed. There was no way of me avoiding collision with this car at the speed I was going and the limited space. Seconds before I was about to collide with the car, I noticed an empty handicap parking spot to my left. I turned on a dime to avoid hitting that car but at the speed I was going all that inertia caused me to fly off the bike losing control. It was almost as if time slowed down while I was in the air, I noticed my head was directly in the path of the handicap sign. My body slowly rotated, next thing I know I heard and felt a sensation of ice being crunched as my right shoulder took the impact instead of my head. The car drove on and I laid there momentarily with a sensation of fire setting into my shoulder, before I could process the pain an employee of the store approached me. "Do you need an ambulance". I don't have insurance and I would rather not create an ambulance bill, I replied no. Unfortunately, I'm going to have to ask you to get off our property, the employee stated. Pain was starting to set in at this point, I asked to use a phone. I called my mom till exhausted with no replies, I decided to get back on my bike and pedaled back home with my right arm dangling sending sharp pain with any movement I made cycling with my less dominate hand. Eventually I made it back home, soon as I walk in the house, I see my mother watching T.V. and noticed she was high so I didn't bother asking why she didn't answer the phone. I think I broke my shoulder, before I could tell her what happened she stopped me saying, "your shoulder is not broke, go lay down". I went in my room trying to position myself on the bed in a way that wasn't too painful. I was not successful, I started crying as most of my adrenaline was likely gone and the pain intensified. Soon as tears fell from my eyes my mom said, "C'mon were going to the hospital". My mother must have followed me to my room because I did not cry loudly. Summer vacation was over and the school year was here once again. "Great!" As I sarcastically thought to myself, I have to walk around the school wearing a sling. It wasn't all bad though, the school provided me a writing assistant to take notes in class for me. As I reviewed the notes given to me after each class, I noticed I unconsciously inherited some of their writing techniques and effective note taking styles. It wouldn't be till my next school that I learned what a GPA was though. Needless to say, but yet another transition in neighborhoods is about to occur.

In a new neighborhood but this time I was reacquainted with the school district that my previous teacher asked me to be the assistant girls basketball coach. I recognized a lot of familiar faces in that neighborhood and became acquainted with new ones as well. This is the summer vacation going into my sophomore year at high school. I would like to thank you again for reading and forewarn that things get more explicit in content as with life. "Yo Borne! You gotta come to this girl house!" What's so special about her house? I replied. Unfortunately, easily influenced by my environment still at that point I ended up in her house. "Her room right there just go in". Soon as I opened the door, I see her having sex and the dude yells get out. I didn't completely understand why I was even in there so as I'm about to leave, the dude that yelled get out stops me and tells me that she wants to suck you. She leads me into her room telling me she doesn't usually suck anyone she must like me. She stops sucking me and says she wants to sit on it, I quickly realized what she meant after she slid myself into her. I'm not proud to admit this but I went back over her house frequently never using a condom.

//Acknowledging the start of my first sexual encounter is import in order to learn from my past that created flawed habits with women. Seeing and reading my own content, is impactful on another scale as I continue to learn and commit to not making the same mistakes again. I hope you the reader can learn from my mistakes as well and not go through the dumb decisions did .//

When summer vacation ended and I entered my sophomore year I decided to join our school's fraternity Theta Phi Psi. We use to have parties of which girls would approach me and my frat brothers wanting to hook up after the party. One of them even asked if she could switch from my frat brother to me after they were finished. These experiences are the precursors as to my less than faithful relationships in the past.

I got my schedule for classes eager to see if I have any classes with any of my teammates, as I played football at this school as well. I shared some classes with my teammates but more importantly I was place in Honors English. This can't be right, I instantly went to the regular English class only to be kicked out and directed back to the honors class. Honors English was not as hard as I thought it would be, it even turned out to be fun. I remember we had a project where we had to in pairs read a book, create a website on it and give a presentation to the class. I was paired with a Korean girl and our book we were assigned was Beowulf. We read the book, created a great website for it, now all that was left was our presentation. We recited in alternate unison taking turns regurgitating what we remembered from the book. We made it through our presentation with a breeze and all that was left was Q and A. One of our classmates asked a question and my partner started answering and then looked at me stopped and gave an indifferent smile showing teeth with her eyes open wide. I took this gesture as she was lost with words to answer the question so I chimed in. I stated everything I previously said but altered a few words in answering their question. I felt like I wasn't answering the questions correctly but I looked over at our teacher and she smiled. She must have enjoyed our comradery and efforts because we received an A. She had a policy where at the end of the semester if you had an A in the class, you could miss three days of her class and not have to take the exam. If you had a B, you could miss two days and if a C only one day. I tallied up in my head and realized I missed 4 days of her class. Prepared to take her final, I walked into her classroom up to her desk. She looked at me gave a wink saying you only missed three days you don't have to take the final. She was one of many great teachers at that school. As football season ended, I transitioned into track and field naturally. On the bus traveling back to our school after one of our track meets, there were some teammates adamant on playing cupid with me and cheesecake. I nicknamed her cheesecake because she was very light skinned. She was a grade under me but she attended the same middle school where I was her assistant basketball coach. She did not carry herself as previous girls I hooked up with, completely innocent in my eyes. I was honored and nervous that she liked me to the point allowing me to be the one to take her virginity. I wanted to treat her different from the past girls I messed with and made sure every time we had sex, we used a condom. My moral compass was half way working as I did try to offer my best self at the time but temptation from parties I went to led me to cheat on her. The next school day word had reached to me that one of my friends snuck out stole his mom's car and was grounded for a while. After that school day ended and the sun was completely gone, I thought to myself I'm sneaking out tonight. Soon as I was certain my mom and her boyfriend were sleep, I snuck out taking my mom's keys and went to pick up one of my friends who asked if he could drive to pick up his girl. Before you know it, all three of us snuck out the house with absolutely no agenda at all. On the highway I suggested we sneak into my house and that became the destination. As my friend was driving, the car slowly came to a stop… Out of gas. "Borne how da hell you forget to put gas in the car!" my friend yelled. "Bruh I don't know, I thought when the gas light come on that means you got 30 miles left". He got out frustrated and started walking to the nearest gas station. Just great! I thought sarcastically, just leave me with your upset girl cursing me out every minute till he returned. We finally made it back to my house, we snuck in, went to my room and I fell asleep watching a movie. Later woken up by them we snuck back out and everyone made it back home safely. These late-night ventures would add to my driving experience required because my mother would move us yet again into a gated community where occasionally I would wake up early drive her to work and drive myself to school.

My mom's boyfriend during this time was a pretty good guy in my eyes. I really only noticed four things from him. He worked, cooked, cleaned and occasionally played video games. He would even take me to empty parking lots and let me practice driving his car in preparation of me obtaining my drivers learner's permit. The main thing I took away from him looking back is when I live with my girlfriend/wife I will make any efforts to try to make her life easier in any way I am able. Having a good male role model was never a constant variable for me. This void would occasionally be filled sometimes thru me spending the night over at friends/frat brothers. Two of my frat brothers whom actually are related to each other by blood always seemed to have a room for me in their home. Their father made me do choirs I've never done before. I remember on one occasion we could not leave the house until we all properly tied a tie.

The next schedule I got for the start of the next semester surprises me yet again. AP Psychology, the principal must be playing with me. Why am I in an AP class? I had no care for achieving a college credit while in high school. Even though it turned out that I really enjoyed the class, I cheated on every test. I honestly believe the teacher was letting me cheat as I was the only dummy using a calculator in a psychology class. I would hide flash cards on the backside of the TI-83 and positioned it to where I believed she could not see the note cards. If I did not care about the class, I would not have put forth the effort of studying and cheating to make sure I accurately answered the questions and essay sections. It was maybe a week or two weeks into my senior year when I was notified that if I take one more technical class that I would be inducted into the National Technical Honor Society.

The idea grew on me and I believed the principal was happy of my interest because my schedule was adjusted even though it was past the add/drop period. I decided to take broadcasting and learned the mechanics and process of recording/editing our announcement throughout the school day. Before I knew it, it was over, graduation was here.

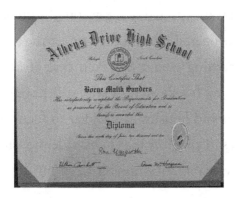

Just to think I was told by doctors I may never be able to walk or talk again and here I am running track at a collegiate level, before I got to this point though I had college scouts watching me in high school. It was my very last track meet at regionals and I was told everything would be taken care of school wise and I would have a place on the track team at NCCU if I could run the 400m under a certain time. Normally I would gage and determine my pace based off the competition then in the last stretch give an all-out burst of speed in the last 100m of the race. Soon as I heard the gun shot to start the race this time I held nothing back out the gate. I threw caution to the wind and there seemed to be a perfect gust of wind blowing against my back propelling me faster than I ever ran before. I finished second but I secured a place on the team running the exact time that was expected of me accomplishing the task. Time goes on and I grew bored under the impression that everything would be taken care of at NCCU, but only my books were, I was still responsible for meal plan and housing. I decided to focus more on academics in an effort to get an academic scholarship and got valuable information from my advisor that

I should consider becoming an Officer in the Air Force. I took my advisor's advice.

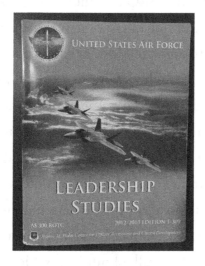

I joined AFROTC while simultaneously being a math tutor on campus. In addition, I also crossed Omega Psi Phi during this time period which is a non-hazing fraternity.

I will not write on the experience or the process of my time in AFROTC but I did graduate field training. I did not know exactly what I wanted to be then; I thought the idea of spec ops would be of my interest though. I had no blood thirst to kill, more so a desire to be an agent to gather valuable intel. My first girlfriend in college during this time period gave me a week to get being a Q dog out my system (partying etc...) which I misinterpreted at the time as a pass to allow my surroundings to persuade me to cheat. I remember I asked her if she trusts me and I proceed to pull a knife out, sat it on my desk, duct taped her hands together, blind folded her and told her to meet me outside so we can go somewhere to eat and I walked out the door. Unconsciously I was trying to free her of my imperfections I grew accustomed to. I started drinking, smoking, partying more and started noticing things in my class that I can't completely explain.

There was this girl that nicknamed me her "headache" amongst all my cheating I contracted herpes. When I first started hearing voices, I remember hearing, "You know you going to hell for this right?" right before I had unprotected sex with the girl whom nicknamed me "headache". Before I climaxed, I pulled out and ejaculated on her stomach, she turned my sperm bloody. I did not realize I had sex with her on her period; the only thing I could think is how am I going to tell her I have herpes. My grades started to fall, I got in a big argument with my granddad, I stopped with Air Force ROTC, my granddad passed shortly after our argument and I was beginning to lose a hold of everything.

Borne Malik Sanders

I began stealing again, another trait from being a product of my past environments that were catching up to me. I knew where all the blind spots were in this store I would steal from because there were no cameras. My schizophrenia played a role as a factor to being able to tell secret shoppers through conversations but I got careless and reckless during the holidays. Normally I would only steal essentials (food, etc..) which still is not good. It was around Christmas time and I began getting greedy wanting to get enough money for presents by pawning what I stole from the store. Long story short, I got caught one day. I got a lawyer and believed the best course of action was to pay the estimated total amount of what I stole accumulatively in efforts for charge to be a misdemeanor. My mother then helped me get the misdemeanor expunged.

Before my first mental breakdown which led me to mental visits in hospitals, the girl which I misinterpreted what she meant by a "week" got me flight lessons for one of my birthdays which was very symbolic because I stopped with AFROTC. Still not knowing how to speak on my status, I gave her herpes on her birthday after she got me in the air with flight lessons... Ill never forgive myself for not being able to speak and gather everything I needed to say at the appropriate time. My schizophrenia got to the point where it was unbearable. I would get on my laptop and play multiple browsers of cartoons in German, French, Farsi, Hindu, Chinese, any language I could think simultaneously so I could drown out voices I could understand but to no avail. I tried praying during this time period and heard no response from God or his angels which baffled me to no end considering I'm schizophrenic. I acquired more than ever an irrational logic that I hope is not understood or repeated that I need to punish myself in the dumb action of spilling blood cutting myself. I kept in and out of rages of which suicide became my only comfortable thought. This led to multiple trips to the hospital in the mental unit from failed attempts taken too far. Someone from my past high school who I thought we were boys took advantage of me. I was drugged and raped. During this lowest I thought I could feel for myself as a result I put rat poison in tea and drank it in efforts to destroy all sins I've committed and all that were committed to me. I wrote a note trying to explain before my appointment with death.

Nothing happened after drinking the tea and 3 main diagnosis were attached to my mental records. Schizophrenia, anxiety, and major depression. Shortly afterwards being released from the hospital's mental unit I remember hearing a female voice while I was on my laptop saying, "That would be worth seeing right?". That voice prompted me to discover that it was exactly a week away from a lunar eclipse during this time period. This was also the time period where I got accepted into NCSU but shortly dropped out because

35

my past mistakes and being taken advantage of results in me never being able to really function well in the parameters of schizophrenia, anxiety, and major depression. This led to my 2nd or 3rd visit to a mental unit in the hospital for quiet a duration over time.

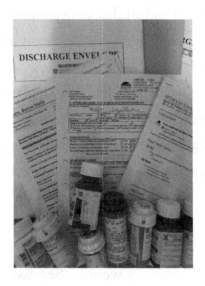

Before this point though, shortly after I pledged and crossed Omega Psi Phi, there was a party/ kickback of which a couple girls wanted to spend the night at the place I lived with some of my frat brothers. I would hear comments like "we are for the campus" from women who wanted to be pleased. These comments clouded and entangled in my mind so I asked one of the girls that came to stay if she wanted to see my room. We made it to my room and she tells me we don't have to do anything. That relieved me because I did not like what I was becoming. She told me she was hungry so we went back downstairs watched TV while I made her ramen noodles. Shortly after the night ended a different girl that also stayed over that night filed a rape charge but the girl I was with validated that I was with her the whole night so my name was clear. I still had to go downtown for questioning. I was led to a room where the police officers left me for a while so I pulled out my phone. I deleted every voice memo I had recorded to make more room for storage then soon as I pressed record and put my phone back in my jacket the interrogation began about the room I never went in that the allegations came from. I later gave the recorded memo audio from my interrogation to some of my frat brothers whom were subject of the questioning.

It may have been my 5th or 6th visit to the mental facility at the hospital from another failed attempt at suicide. I totaled my old car from crashing it into a bus.

Your Motor Vehicle Record (traffic violations and accident history) was used to determine your rate. Your Motor Vehicle Record adversely affected your rate and was based on the following information contained in the Motor Vehicle Record:

DRIVER NAME	INCIDENT	INCIDENT/CONVICTION DATE
Borne Sanders	Speeding over 10 MPH Over Posted Speed that is less than 55 MPH; Speeding in a School Zone; Speeding (No Speed Given)	10/05/2019
Borne Sanders	Speeding Over 10 MPH Over Posted Speed provided speed is >55 but <76 MPH	09/10/2019
Borne Sanders	At-Fault PD $3,850+	04/17/2019

The consumer reporting agency played no part in the decision to take this action with respect to your insurance and will be unable to give you the specific reasons for what we did.

You have the right to request a free copy of your consumer report from the consumer reporting agency. Your request must be made within 60 days of receiving this notice. You also have the right to dispute with the consumer reporting agency the accuracy or completeness of any information in your consumer report. Please note: we played no role in the makeup of your consumer report.

You may contact the consumer reporting agency by writing or calling them at the following address:

For Consumer Credit Information
Consumer Disclosure
PO Box 1000
Chester, PA 19022
1-800-645-1938
www.transunion.com

01815 (03012019)

Only thing, this visit was peculiarly shorter than previous visits. There were maybe 6 police officers and someone qualified to give shots gave me an injection then I was placed in a strafe jacket and taken away to the mental facility. They took my phone and wallet and soon as I was checked into the mental unit I was released within the same day. I still had a one problem though, no phone or wallet. I spent a lot of my time under a bridge after failing to reach anyone at a hotel that allowed me to use their phone. Most of the night goes by and after no positive attempts at sleep, laying on the concrete, I got up and started walking and a flashback of which direction I needed to go came into play and I set off on foot. It was maybe halfway through my travel when I decided to take off my slippers because they were rubbing badly were I suffered a foot injury from football. One day at football practice I was running full speed and my left foot hit the back of one of my teammate's cleeks. I hyperextended my left big toe and then later my right big toe as well. Meaning both toes popped out of the joint and popped back in. I began to get a blister walking home on my left toe which was injured worst. The more I walked, the more the side of the slipper began to cut so I began to walk barefoot. The sun was starting to rise and I was maybe 3/4th of the way home when a truck stopped in front of me. This white man I would say maybe in his 40's asked if I needed a ride. Spending a lot of time walking I came to the rationalization that this was maybe the outcome I deserve from my previous dumb actions and denied

the offer of a ride. I felt emersed in depression that this was the police and hospital way of sending me a message. The man in the truck happened to have shoes and socks that were my size. He gave them to me and I still own them to this day.

I value this lesson because past experiences from previous mental unit visits annoyed reality of what had to be a routine under their protocols/rules/ supervision. Every night at one of the hospitals they would open your door and flash a red laser directly at your eyes at intervals that only seemed to occur as soon as your about to drift off to sleep. Reason being they gave was everyone had to be on the same frequency. Then they would hold group therapy sessions early in the morning and if you were not present it would hurt your chances of being discharged. Morning time was the only time I could sleep peacefully though because that's when the night staff wasn't annoying us with red lasers.

The sun would rise and set more times than I can count but the day never seemed to change for me. I could not escape my depression from reflecting on what my experiences have made me and the fact that I was drugged and raped. I began recording and releasing music to YouTube as a way to try to heal myself. The more I expressed myself through music the worst my schizophrenia got from hearing conversations relating to the content of my work. No matter how well I tried to explain this to doctors, it would always be taken out of context. The best way I could describe this pain I wrote lyrics for and recorded a song.

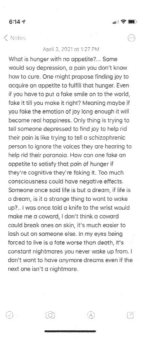

My mother would occasionally visit me at the apartment I was staying at during this time period. She brought our dog during one of her visits. I was listening to one of my songs where I was verbally attacking myself from every angle. I had my headphones on and when she handed me Chloe's kennel and belongings, I sat them both down opened her kennel for her to go potty and immediately went in my apartment to put up her belongings. When I returned back outside, I witnessed the aftermath of my mother running over Chloe with her car. I was devastated, Chloe was more than a dog. She was my little sister. The only thing I could muster to say was, "why did you kill Chloe?". I did not want to see or speak to my mother after that happened. Before Chloe's death I visited my mother at her place. When I got there Chloe was sleeping in her kennel. When she woke up and realized it was me on the couch, she got excited and tried to jump on the couch with me and my mom. My mom told her to get down and normally I would ignore comments like that from my mother and pick Chloe up anyway because she was a house dog. That visit I did not ignore my mother for some reason I ignored Chloe. I feel if I wouldn't have ignored Chloe and treated her how I normally do that she would have stayed on my heels and not have followed my mother to her death.

Immediately after her death I got tattoos in honor of her that signified to me that from the moment I touched her, she found her way up my arm and made it to my heart.

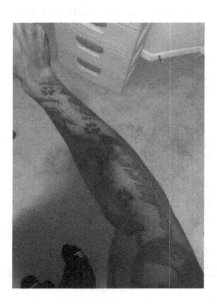

For quite some time I did not want to speak to my mother. After more time passed she expressed to me that she has found a relationship with God and would like for me to embark with her. I always believed that a God has to exist after all how was earth created? Scientist may have a rebuttal holding on to the Big Bang Theory, but in my eyes, God is energy. The Big Bang was God's energy. I never had a close relationship with God growing up but I thank my mother dearly for showing/teaching me how to build a relationship with God. I have had a lot of pain that disabled me mentally and my mother has helped greatly with mentally disabling my pain. My name is Borne Malik Sanders and thank you for reading.

Printed in the United States
by Baker & Taylor Publisher Services